THE HISTORY OF THE TOPPER DINGHY AND ITS CLASS ASSOCIATION

Roger Cleland has been associated with Toppers since 1983 and his first Nationals at Kessingland. Since 1988 he has taken part as a parent, North West Representative, Vice Chairman, Chairman, International Chairman and Commodore in 13 Nationals and six World Championships. Racing in the North West amongst a handful of other parents, he was known as the "Silver Fox" but truthfully his main rival was "Mrs. Silver Fox". For 37 years he taught French at Altrincham Grammar School for Boys, the last ten as Deputy Headmaster. He retired from teaching in 2004 and now sails a Hunter 27 from Pwllheli.

THE HISTORY OF THE TOPPER DINGHY AND ITS CLASS ASSOCIATION

Roger Cleland

Pitchpole Books

Cheshire

ISBN 978-0-9575549-6-2

Published by
Pitchpole Books
Cheshire, England
2016

To Jennifer, Mrs Silver Fox

CONTENTS

ILLUSTRATIONS

ACKNOWLEDGEMENTS

A number of people have helped in putting this history together to whom I owe my sincere thanks. Some have given me access to archive material, notably the current ITCA(GBR) secretary, Jeanette Sanderson, who has lent me past copies of Topper Times and other relevant papers and who has patiently dealt with my mithering enquiries.

My thanks to the Proctor family for the photographs of early Toppers, to Topper International Ltd for those of manufacturing and to Dave Cockerill for that of the 4.2 sail.

The remainder of the photographs are from Topper Times and are reproduced with the permission of the ITCA(GBR) committee. For most of these the individual photographers are not known but where they are I acknowledge them. To the others I just say thank you..

Roger Proctor has been most encouraging in the undertaking of the whole project and has given his permission for the reproduction of one of his articles in Topper Times and of those of his father, Ian. Rather than tinker around with his early history, I have reprinted it in full for the first two chapters and added extracts from an article by Martin Fry on Topper production, again sometimes verbatim.

I also thank those who have vetted pen-portraits, offered photographs and volunteered their viewpoint on various matters, particularly Graham Wright, Jonathan Cunnison, Dave Cockerill (for the reproduction of photographs from "The Topper Book"), Harry Brown, Helen and Alan Evans and Derek Burchell whose long association with the class helped enormously to bridge the gap in my experience and knowledge.

The Topper Class owes a huge debt of gratitude to literally hundreds of adults who have taken on the responsibility of a position on the Committee or pitched in as assistant measurers, sail number appliers for hired boats and extra safety boat crews for large events. Without you, there would be no Class and certainly not the success that this history catalogues.

It is always invidious to pick out individuals from so many: Ian Proctor pays tribute to Geoff Wright in chapter 1 and I think one other person stands out – Chris Robinson – who in his quietly unassuming manner but steely resolve and legal expertise steered the Class through a tricky legal issue.

I am extremely grateful in addition to Roger Proctor who not only cast a critical eye over a draft version but who kindly wrote the Foreword to this book.

My friend and Pitchpole Books publisher, Geoff Meggitt, has provided essential editorial assistance, has made a large contribution to the design and generally encouraged me throughout. I also thank my wife, Jennifer, for proof reading the text.

FOREWORD

When Roger Cleland first suggested that he write a history of the Topper I thought it would be simple, just gather a few articles, old copies of Topper Times and string them all together. Well, as is often the case with these things, it is never that simple.

The story of the Topper is an incredible one really, and very well told by Roger.

It starts with Ian Proctor and a concept – to design a simple, cheap, 'friendly' boat that could get people of all ages into sailing – a sport he loved and he felt delivered mental and physical agility, self reliance, independence, fun and sportsmanship.

But then a new dynamic comes into play – along comes someone who believes that Britain can lead the world in polypropylene plastics technology and has a vision. So Maurice Robin and my father get together, become firm friends, and with a shared passion sell the idea of a boat moulded using a process pushed beyond its known technical limits that may have, if it works, a huge impact on the future of the UK's plastics industry and beyond. And they manage to persuade the National Enterprise Board, Guinness and ICI to back the project.

So it all comes together to create a boat, a technology and approach that has a worldwide reputation that still flourishes today. Indeed I am told that in the plastics engineering industry the Topper has legendary status, with the Open University still featuring the story as part of their engineering degree courses.

One of the most gratifying experiences for us as a family was in 2012 going to the V&A and the Science Museums to see the Topper exhibited next to the E-Type Jaguar and Concorde in exhibitions to showcase the best of British

Design from 1945-2012 and the Best of British Manufacturing, respectively.

So it is a story of design and technology, but that is only half of the story. The other half is the story of people, the story of their faith, commitment, hard work vision, passion and skill.

These are the people who have either been sailors themselves or who have supported their children as sailors. Travelled the miles, slept in their cars, committed their lives to the circuit, racing and training in all weathers at all times of the year, in the UK and abroad.

It is also the people who have devoted themselves to helping build and maintain the class, training, coaching, running safety, finance, writing the rules, child protection, results, measurement – the list is endless. Their selfless commitment is beyond measure.

Added to this are also the people who manufacture the boat, form the class committees around the world, indeed travel the world talking about and promoting the boat to national sailing authorities, sailing clubs and international committees.

This is all very humbling and one should reasonably ask why, why do they do it? It is something I constantly wonder and worry about, but I think I may just have found the answer.

You see it is those faces, those happy smiling faces of the sailors.

It is the fortitude and skill that they develop, the confidence and independence they show, the intelligence and physical fitness they demonstrate. And above all it is the sportsmanship they advertise. They are part of our best, they give us hope for the future. And the humble Topper manages to play a catalytic and positive role in their people's lives, both old and young, and parents and children.

So the Topper can never be considered in isolation. It is at its basic level a piece of polypropylene, a lump of plastic. But it is a medium that has gathered around it a huge group of amazing people who do amazing things for each other, their families and the sport we all love, sailing.

It is these people that are the Topper.

Roger Proctor

PREFACE

You may wonder why anyone, particularly someone who has been away from the Topper scene for a decade, should want to write the history of the boat, its Class Association and its huge development into one of the current RYA's "Pathway" boats when so much information is on the ITCA (GBR) website. The trouble is the website only presents the facts and even so only goes back a short while rather than to the beginning with no explanation on how things happened and why changes were made.

There have been books on "Topper Sailing" by John Caig and an updated version by John and Dave Cockerill and a book on "Topper Racing" by Donnie Meldrum, but these are primarily "how to do" books with only a passing reference to the Topper's history. The account I present of the Class Association will hopefully appeal to past Topper sailors and set the Topper into the context of where the boat and its Association is today. At the same time, I hope some of the myths that are apt to have taken hold through want of a full history can be dismissed and the record be put right.

Obviously in ploughing through dozens and dozens of Topper Times and questioning past officials and sailors it is abundantly clear that there have been hundreds of sailors whose names are not mentioned and yet who have contributed hugely to the Topper story in their own way. Please do not be offended – no slight is intended – but rather enjoy the satisfaction of being able to say, "I was there".

It is often tempting to look back nostalgically and think that your particular era was the best. Of course it is impossible to compare and therefore know, but it's a healthy sign that each generation is gaining its maximum enjoyment for this to be considered the case.

Roger Cleland, Lymm, January 2016

1: CONCEPTION AND BIRTH

L et us start at the beginning of the history of the Topper to discover how the original concept was developed into the boat that we know today. In the summer of 1987, Ian Proctor wrote an account of the early years of the Topper in Topper Times which gives us a comprehensive narrative of the early design, production and evolution of the boat and which I gratefully reproduce here with the kind permission of the designer's family.

THE EARLY YEARS

"In 1969 George O'Day, an American for whom I had previously designed two International 14-ft dinghies and who had won a gold medal in 5.5 metres in the Olympics, asked me to design a single-handed boat for the North American market. At that time he was President of the O'Day Corporation, which was one of the largest sailboat organisations in the U.S.A. and they were building my International Tempest design, which was currently one of the Olympic keelboat classes. Proctor Masts were also supplying him with a lot of masts. He knew the Minisail, which is one of my designs of which there were then about 5,000, and wanted the new boat to be in roughly the same category, but left all the other decisions to me.

Naturally the first thing to do was to study the market. There seemed to be a potential worldwide market for the kind of boat I had in mind and it was decided that George should look after North America and the Caribbean, while I tried to spread the new class through the rest of the world, including of course the UK.

We had a Minisail in my family and it was great fun, but hard work in a breeze and the younger helmsmen became overpowered in fresh winds, so that the boat tended to take charge and was not always properly under control. It is always tempting to make high performance a top priority, but much more difficult to produce a boat that is well mannered

1

and easy to control, as well as being a reasonable performer. The main objective of this new project was to produce a boat that would appeal to the widest possible range of helmsmen – not demanding too much weight or strength, being suitable for young people and girls as well as everyone else, safe for the inexperienced but not boring to the expert, with good manners under the widest possible range of conditions.

Obviously this meant less sail area than the Minisail, requiring less strength and weight to control it. But small sail area on a relatively large hull is like putting a low powered engine into a large car – the result is dull and frustrating. So the Topper's hull was reduced to a size that would make a good stable platform for the rig, but small enough to react with spirit to the drive from the small sail area.

A boat that is intended to be sailed all over the world, often by those who may not have sailed much before, should be simple and the use of its gear as obvious as possible. Instruction books soon get lost, are often in the wrong language anyway, and are seldom passed on beyond the first owner. Such things as sail battens are easily lost or broken and a sail that is designed to be used with battens is hopelessly inefficient and quickly ruined without them. A sleeved sail is simple, and had been used on the Minisail for many years, but it cannot easily be lowered and the mast is hard to put up or down with a battened sail unfurled and flapping like a great flag – so that is another reason for not having battens. A kicker is a great aid to controllability and in its original form on the Topper was simple and fairly obvious in use.

There are other controls on the Topper, but they are all of a kind that do not cause disaster if their proper use is a mystery to the user and they are maladjusted, though of course performance suffers. The objective of many of the class rules is to preserve this principle of simplicity, which I am sure is of paramount importance to the long-term future of the class.

Those were the main guidelines behind the design. George O'Day wanted a prototype built to prove them so, as well as the round bilge hull that we now use, I designed a hard-chine version as a cheap trial horse. Sailing trials were eagerly conducted by the younger members of the Proctor family. Nothing needed changing and patterns for the production hull and deck were started immediately, under my supervision. The original idea was for the hull and deck to be 'cold-press' moulded in GRP in the UK and shipped to the USA. Cold-press moulding is a little like the injection moulding process now used, because the skin is produced between two moulds under pressure, but it is a much slower and involves more labour, and the only heat involved is exotherm generated by the chemical reaction of the resin. Not so much pressure is needed and therefore the moulds are far cheaper, but still a lot more costly than moulds for normal hand-laid GRP. As this method was still in the development stage, it was decided to begin with conventional hand-moulded hulls to save time.

In addition to the original USA licence, other builders were soon licenced in Israel and Austria. The class was called 'OD11'. The Israeli builders were particularly active, selling more than 2,000 in the first three years to 16 countries, so cold-pressed production was shelved for the time being and soon further licences were issued in Australia, Spain and Africa. Before long 4,500 of these boats were spread around the world.

John Dunhill, who was establishing a modest boatbuilding business in the early seventies only a few hundred yards from where the cold-press GRP operation was planned, saw the unused moulds, contacted me, applied for the UK licence and got it. An Israeli boat was supplied to him as a guide to the finished product. He did not like the name 'OD11' and the much jauntier and more appropriate name of 'Topper' was adopted instead. (the name was first suggested by Jill Davies (née Proctor) during a family discussion around the kitchen table).

In summer 1973 I entered an Israeli-built Topper in Yachting World's One-of-a-Kind Beachboat Rally with a young helmsman. It did conspicuously well and received very favourable press comments. Thereafter the boat met with increasing success in the UK. At the following London Boat Show, John Dunhill was approached on his stand by the Managing Director of Rolinx, a subsidiary of I.C.I., who said he had just developed a method of producing very large polypropylene injection mouldings. He wanted to demonstrate this method commercially. The Topper was the ideal product to publicise the method and a set of mouldings could be turned out every seven minutes. Was John interested?

Hotfoot, they came round to see me on the Proctor Mast stand. Of course I was excited about the idea too, but the Topper Class was already going well, with the prospect of more overseas builders being established soon, and I thought it might be better to design a new boat altogether, rather than interfere with the already assured progress of the Topper. I thought it would be difficult to make polypropylene Toppers exactly the same as those in GRP. I had just written the class rules, which were intended to keep the Topper a strict one-design, and I was sure this was of utmost importance for its future.

Anyway, the next week John and I flew to Manchester and visited the Rolinx factory. The Managing Director, Maurice Robin, was a brilliant engineer and a great enthusiast for new ideas. He assured me that one of his chief objectives was to demonstrate to the plastics world that they could produce an injection moulded polypropylene boat virtually exactly the same as the GRP version and for that very reason, above nearly all others, he wanted to produce the Topper as it was – and not a new boat. So I agreed. After all, the class was growing well in GRP and if the new material was not successful we could always go back to GRP.

Many technical problems came up, some of them connected with the large allowances required to accommodate the great shrinkage of polypropylene when it cools after moulding. But Maurice Robin was true to his word and often when I offered to change something to make things easier, he would say that it was his job to find a way round. I think he really enjoyed technical problems, though he may not have been so keen on the financial ones. We became very firm friends. The Topper was his swan song and he retired immediately the project was completed, and he died soon afterwards. Things changed after that.

Some re-design work was necessary of course, and while I was doing that the Directors of Rolinx and John Dunhill set about raising the £250,000 (at 1973 values) required for the new metal mould tools. Fortunately a very senior executive in the Guinness Group was already the enthusiastic owner of two Toppers (this was before the Ernest Saunders era) and John contacted him – with the result that Guinness provided half the tooling costs and eventually took over John Dunhill's boat company. The other half of the tooling costs were contributed by the National Research and Development Corporation (since disbanded) which felt that the project was not only viable, but of great importance to the prestige of British plastics technology. We were on our way, but it was another two years before we would see a polypropylene Topper.

While the complicated metal moulds were being made there was time for some refinements to be designed, such as the rudder, tiller, daggerboard, mast gate and the mast and boom fittings. But we had many meetings to discuss problems like joining the hull and deck together and we had no answer to this particular problem until very near the date for production to start. Polypropylene will not take adhesives and we considered high frequency welding, riveting, everything, but nothing was satisfactory. Then I remembered that years before I had visited a furniture firm that were going to manufacture one of my wooden boats and they incorporated a thin wire in some of their furniture's glue joints and passed an electric current through it to hasten the curing of the adhesive locally, so that the piece of furniture was just strong enough to be lifted off the production line and stored until the whole glue joint had cured properly. I wondered if the jointing surfaces of the hull and deck could be heated in the same way, so that the polypropylene surfaces fused together. So I mentioned it and before long Rolinx had developed the copper/polypropylene braid which goes around the gunwale, between the hull and deck mountings, and through which the current is passed to fuse the whole thing together. We had a particularly good lunch after that meeting.

As soon as the first polyprop boat was put together it was brought down to my home on the Hamble River and we had trials, though the new rudder and tiller were not finished. No real problems, so we were ready for the launch of the polyprop Topper."

1: Early Toppers:

Clockwise from top left: wooden, two fibreglass boats, polyprop.

IAN PROCTOR was born in 1918, and had a most distinguished career. He learned to sail at Gresham's School in Holt, Norfolk, taking advantage of the Norfolk Broads. During the war he abandoned his studies at medical school to join the Royal Air Force Volunteer Reserve and served in an air sea rescue unit in the Mediterranean.

Invalided out of the RAF through polio, he turned his attention to writing about sailing in the "Yachtsman" and then as the sailing correspondent for the "Daily Telegraph". Successful as a sailor himself winning several National titles in various boats, he is best known for developing tapered aluminium alloy masts (Proctor metal masts became world renowned) and for a prolific career as a yacht designer. Over the years he produced scores and scores of boats many of which are still sailed regularly today, including the Gull, Wayfarer, Wanderer, Bosun, Kestrel, Minisail and of course the Topper – probably his most commercially successful boat and one which won him numerous design awards for its innovation. He died in 1992 aged 74 at a Wayfarer World Championship at Hayling Island.

In paying tribute to Ian, Chris Robinson (TICA (UK) Commodore) wrote in Topper Times "Countless are the hours which he gave us collectively whether in committee or at events both home and abroad. His experience of sailing and its administration was of the highest order and this he was able to bring to bear quietly, courteously and at times with enormous patience as we sought to steer through sometimes very troubled waters. He had a great sense of humour and an infectious chuckle with which he was usually able to take the heat out of potentially difficult situations and achieve a satisfactory conclusion. To the officers of the class he was always available and was a tower of strength at times of trouble."

2: INTO POLYPROP

Continuing Ian Proctor's account of the early history of the Topper.

" The launch of the polyprop Topper in autumn 1975 was a grand occasion, with lots of press. We had planned to drop a Topper from car-top height onto concrete, to show how strong it was. We had a rehearsal to check that it wouldn't split, but we held our breath as the photographers lined up, hoping that a second drop would not be too much for it. It dropped and was fine – everyone was tremendously impressed except for one character cursing at his flash gun that had not fired. It was dropped twice more before that chap got his picture. It was nerve wracking, to say the least, but good propaganda.

Of course the production of hull and deck mouldings in Manchester did not complete the task, and an assembly line was set up at a light engineering plant in Cornwall that belonged to Guinness. The sales organization was in Hampshire. It never impressed me as an ideal arrangement.

The polyprop Topper was shown to the public for the first time at the 1976 London Boat Show and although it created a lot of interest, it was met with a good deal of suspicion as well. Nobody associated polypropylene with boats, though they knew it was used for dustbins and washing-up bowls, so it was natural that many should put the new Topper in the same category.

This new method of manufacture demanded a completely different marketing technique. The great cost of tooling and setting up the initial run of mouldings had to be recovered fairly quickly. This meant publicising and advertising on a scale that had only been seen in the Mirror, Enterprise and Laser classes previously. Before long the suspicion of polypropylene began to fade away and in 1977 Topper received a Design Council Award and a year later the Horner Award from the plastics industry, the top honour for technical development. However, some countries are still suspicious of the material and this has inhibited the growth of the Topper abroad.

It was clear that to help make the heavy investment viable, Dunhill Boats needed as wide a market as possible. The market just was not big enough to share with a number of GRP licencees in various parts of the world, if sufficient Toppers were to be built to enable tooling costs to be recovered. That was not my problem directly, but I had realised that this would be so and had refused several applications for licences in the two previous years. George O'Day had sold his boat building business in the USA. The idea then was to ship unassembled polyprop hulls to strategically placed assembly units abroad, thus saving shipping space and some import duty. Unfortunately this has never been done, though the GRP licences abroad were gradually withdrawn to give the polypropylene boat a world market.

There were ten starters in the first National Championships, held in Langstone Harbour in 1973, three years before the polyprop boat appeared and won by my youngest son, Roger, in an Israeli boat. The next three championships were run from Bosham, in Chichester Harbour – 1974 was won by Ron Hope in near gale conditions; 1975 was won by Bridget Quick at the age of 60. These early results indicated the suitability of Toppers for all ages and weather conditions. The first championship in which polyprop boats sailed with GRP versions was in 1976 – an event won by Wendy Fitzpatrick (an accomplished Laser sailor) from about 40 starters. GRP and polyprop boats shared the honours very evenly, thus clearly demonstrating that the one-design principle had not been shattered by the introduction of the polyprop boats. By 1978 championship entrants had increased to over 100 and henceforth continued to grow.

Many people contributed enormous amounts of time and effort to build up the class organization in those early years and it is difficult to mention a few without leaving out many that richly deserve mention too. However, it is impossible to review the establishment of the Topper Class without stating that it was largely steered into being by Geoff Wright, the first Chairman who kept things on course for many years, often through stormy waters. He then became Secretary of the International Committee and did great work in that role too, in the face of serious difficulties. We have nearly always been extremely fortunate in the Topper officers and Committee members who run the class – indeed I think we are particularly fortunate right now – and I, for one, am extremely grateful to all those who have done so much to make the class the success that it is.

While all this activity was going on in the racing sphere, the Topper was becoming increasingly important as a training boat. Many were bought by Sailing Schools, Education Authorities and Local Authorities and it always pleases me to think that many people are introduced to sailing by the Topper. Many Toppers are used by holiday organisations as well. In fact most of the boats are never used for racing at all, which is something that has to be remembered by TICA (UK) and its Committee.

Though most Topper owners probably did not realise it, there were changes behind the scenes in 1982 that could have proved devastating for the class, or for the polyprop boat at least. John Dunhill had been let go in 1981 from the firm he had started and Guinness, under the new Group Chief, Ernest Saunders, who subsequently achieved notoriety, had decided to sell or liquidate about 140 fringe businesses belonging to the brewing giant. Topper International, as it had been re-named, was one of the last to go. Honnor Marine at Dartington had almost completed the purchase of Topper International when Martin Fry, Chairman of Jeneva International, clinched a rival deal at the unlikely hour of 4a.m. on May 12th, 1983.

A little earlier Rolinx had announced that the minimum run of mouldings that it would produce in future was 2,500 (of each) and the cost of the mouldings would be considerably increased; this made the required investment in a moulding run too high to be practical. Shortly afterwards I.C.I. sold Rolinx. I began strongly to feel that I preferred the simple, straightforward days when boatbuilders had sawdust in their hair and shavings underfoot.

Topper International had sold off nearly all stock before Martin Fry took over and moved the operation to Ashford in Kent. There were only a few Toppers to be had in 1983, but Martin tackled the problem with energy and expertise. In spite of being up till the early hours of the morning that he bought Topper International, he flew down to see me the same day. That impressed me. I had discovered that there were only two injection moulders in Europe, other than Rolinx, who could produce mouldings the size of the Topper – one in France and the other in West Germany. Eventually the moulds that had been produced in the UK, and half paid for by British tax payers' money, had to be shipped to Sulo in Germany, who offered to produce the mouldings more cheaply and in shorter runs. When I thought of the innovative genius and initiative of Maurice Robin who developed the technology for Britain, I was very sad.

However, Topper International Ltd. have produced reliable boats to a high standard. When modifications have seemed necessary and practical, they have willingly carried them out. They tackle the overseas market more vigorously and we have seen some good results. Then will be the time to apply for official I.Y.R.U. International status, which would broaden horizons enormously.

It seems as though the Topper has had a chequered and exciting career – and so it has. Sometimes it has caused a few headaches. But the most important thing is for people to enjoy their Toppers in whatever way they wish, whether it is racing, learning, or simply sailing for the fun of it."

To compliment Ian's account, I include here some extracts from a long article that Martin Fry wrote for Topper Times in 2009 on Topper Production. Some highlight the same events in the Topper story but Martin goes into considerable technical detail about tonnage of moulds and clamping forces applied which tend to leave laymen, and this layman in particular, behind. However some statistics are worth mentioning… "In today's money the main tool would cost a staggering £1,000,000 to replace (that's what our insurance company say) and all the other tooling including the daggerboard, the rudder, the tiller and the mastgate, we know would cost a further £200,000." Bearing in mind the cost and sheer size of the machinery involved, it is little wonder that there were so few companies able to undertake injection moulding on this scale.

In April 1983 only Sulo (of dustbin manufacture fame) were able to mould the first of the Toppers under the new ownership of Topper International (bought by Martin from Guinness Leisure) – their first boat being 25000. In 1990 Sulo decided to concentrate on their core business and a firm called Otto took over a new moulding facility in Measham near Derby. Much of the work is done nowadays by robots and the moulding process guarantees a uniformity of strength and quality in both hull and deck. In time Otto reorganized its production empire and moved first to Chalon near Lyon in 1992 and then Neurippin near Berlin in 1998. Lorries transport the mouldings in batches of up to 240 at a time to Ashford in Kent where (here I quote) "the main part of the assembly process consists of welding the hull and decks together. The welding is carried out in a purpose made horizontal jig. After the buoyancy mouldings have been put in place and the bailer hole routed and the gasket installed, welding braid is inserted along the gunwale of the hull and deck mouldings. Transom inner plates and the mast heel gaskets are also installed. The hull and deck are then clamped together. An even join is further ensured with an air gasket. A computer-controlled current cycle is then connected to the braid which in effect fuses the hull to the deck.

The rest of the assembly process consists of a further 30 individual steps including fitting out the hull with toe straps, bailer, transom fittings, mastgate, hull plate and daggerboard mouldings. Last of all the coveted ISAF international Class badge is affixed along with the RYA certified CE plate. The hull is then bubble packed and shrink wrapped depending on its destination and another Topper hull is ready for its new owner."

MARTIN FRY purchased Topper International Ltd. in 1983 from Guinness Leisure who at the time had ceased manufacturing the Topper. The job in hand was to get it all started again. The moulder in Manchester who had been making the Topper was not able to continue, so a new moulder had to be found. After many fruitless enquiries he finally found what we had been looking for in Germany. Since then we have had several stop starts and precipice situations, but they managed to ride the situations and the moulder has moved from Germany to France to the UK and now back to Germany but this time just outside Berlin.

Martin came to sailing quite late when asked to crew in the Albacore Class. This was a good move as the boat did well finishing 2nd twice in the National Championship and also winning the first race in the 1986 World Championship. Since then he has sailed Hurricanes and moved on to helming large catamarans in Turkey and Croatia.

2: Stages of manufacture

3: INTERNATIONAL STATUS

It is quite easy to forget that the earliest fibreglass Toppers were made abroad in Israel and under licence elsewhere and that these boats, numbering some 4,500, were exported around the world to 16 other countries.

The problem was that there was no class coordinating different national groups of boats so the notion of some joint/combined sailing event had no chance of developing, even though some countries may have begun to organise basic racing events. As Britain became in time by far the largest holder of Toppers and by its well structured Class Association, it was best placed to take a lead in promoting international cooperation and recognition.

Although the Class Association was known as TICA (UK) and the "I" being international, it was not recognized by the International Yacht Racing Union as having international status.

It was at the 1987 Annual General Meeting of TICA(UK) at Thorpe Bay that the Class Association was given a mandate to make whatever preparations were necessary for an application to the IYRU for international status for the Topper Class, then to submit that application to the IYRU and to follow it up in whatever way was required to make it successful.

A sub-committee was formed consisting of the Designer, the Builder (or their representatives), Chris Robinson as UK Chairman and Tony Franklin and Geoff Wright with a view to making a submission in early 1989 for consideration at the IYRU meeting that November.

Questions were being asked among Topper members about the significance of such a move when the class was strong in the UK, well run and providing a full programme of racing.

The sub-committee made the case for such a move pointing out the advantages:

15

a) the strict one design made it especially suitable for international racing (it was impossible to buy your way to success as in some other classes)

b) if the boat became very strong in say the USA it would be technically possible that UK control could be lost, though the UK constitution made this unlikely.

c) there are a number of countries where a boat cannot be raced unless it is an international class even though individuals may have bought them because clubs won't include them in their regattas.

The disadvantages were relatively minor. True the IYRU would have to ratify any rule changes and they would levy a small fee on each new boat sold.

The early stumbling block was that any application had to be supported by six National Authorities from three or more continents, each with a minimum of 20 boats. The RYA strongly supported the UK's position but there were problems of interpretation over the UAE being regarded as part of Asia and not Africa. Finland, Latvia and the UK (Europe); Japan, Malaysia, Hong Kong and Singapore (Asia) and crucially Barbados (USA) cemented the bid's criteria.

Backed by the financial support of Topper International Ltd. and the encouragement of the Proctor Design Partnership, plus the input of Bryn Vaile of Matchtight Media and Helen Evans as International Secretary the bid was finally accepted in 1994. Chris Robinson wrote at the time… "I have now discharged the task I was given in 1987 at the request of the late Ian Proctor. I know how pleased he would have been with this result."

This then was seen as the launch pad to encourage each of the countries where Toppers are sailed to establish active Class Associations to promote the development of new fleets. More than a decade later the work still goes on.

An unusual event of a semi-international nature took place in the early 80s and 90s – Ski Topper. The venues changed from Norway to northern France / Switzerland but the format was the same: Topper racing followed by a move to a ski resort nearby for ski races to find a combined champion. Sadly it didn't last for many years, I suspect because Topper sailing abroad was not very well established and so was rather hit and miss.

Tentatively, European Championships were combined with our National Championships in 1979 before being staged abroad in 1980 but they only attracted a handful of foreign entrants, mostly a loyal group of German sailors headed by Elmar Rosemann. World Championships started in 1982 but on a two year cycle until 2008 when it was included in the annual calendar. Depending on where it is held very much determines which foreign countries and how many entrants attend while the British contingent always support in large numbers.

An early foray abroad to try to gain some international experience was for GBR to send a team to the Irish Nationals, initially using borrowed boats, but the following year to transport their own, with greater success.

In 2012 an International Working group was set up to give a boost to Topper Class Associations worldwide and in particular to encourage new outlets in South Africa, South Korea, Madagascar, India and Hawaii. This has now grown to Toppers being present in five continents with the most recent entrants of China, Malta and Thailand. After all it appears that overall 17,000 Toppers have been sold abroad so there is plenty of future scope.

ROGER PROCTOR is the youngest son of Ian and Betty Proctor. Roger is a Director of the family business, Ian Proctor Designs Limited, which was set up to administer Ian's many boat designs after his death in 1992. As such he is the Designer's Representative for the Topper.

Born in 1956, Roger began sailing at a very early age, moving from crewing for his brothers in a Gull and Merlin Rocket to helming a Gull, National 12, Topper, Minisprint and Wanderer. He became the first Topper National Champion in 1973 when it was a much smaller entry than nowadays, and when he was also much smaller!

He developed his love and expertise in capsizing at the tender age of 3 when sailing the prototype Minisail in 1960 on the River Hamble with his brother Keith. What doesn't kill you makes you stronger!

Roger first sailed the prototype wooden Topper (OD11) in 1969, moved on to the fibreglass Israeli version (282) and then finally the Polypropylene version.

Outside of his boating interests he is the founder and Managing Director of Proctor + Stevenson (design and marketing) and Intimis (marketing automation technology). He has wide ranging design interests inherited from his father, with particular emphasis in encouraging greater links between the design industry and education. He advises and talks on design education, chairs and sits on various boards, and was awarded an Honorary Degree by the University of the West of England and given an MBE in recognition of his work with education.

He is married to Gina, lives in Glastonbury, and they have 4 children.

4: CHANGES TO THE BOAT

If the Topper is a one-design boat, has it changed at all over its 50 odd year history? Certainly there have been cosmetic differences in the colour of the decks that different manufacturers have produced. There have been light blue, yellow, dark blue, red, grey, beige, pink and purple decks but not all the colours were as stable as others with a knock resulting in a white mark showing against the colour. Today only red decks are produced. Similarly with the sails which originally were two tone in an alternating colour and white. Over time, blues (light and dark), red, yellow mustard, black, tan, orange, purple, pink and fluorescent yellow panels have featured as long as the sail was predominately white. Today only red and dark blue panels at the foot and red at the head of a white sail is on the market. The white hull has remained the same.

As you would expect, as materials and fittings improved, it will come as no surprise that small changes were made without really affecting its one-design concept.

As early as 1976 the maststep bolt was changed to a cross head bolt which goes through both the hull and the deck. Three years later (at approximately sail number 14450) the Holt Allen self bailer was replaced by the present more efficient IYE bailer and the aluminium cast pintle that screwed into the hull was replaced by the present style stainless-steel transom plate. In 1982 the lightweight sailcloth used in the Gaastra and Danny Robins sails was replaced when Hyde Sails became the official sailmakers. Using a heavier cloth allowed a thicker boom to be introduced to take the added load of mast bend applied through the kicker.

In 1985 a centre toe strap was added, albeit of limited and strictly controlled length, in order to help young sailors maximize their leverage. One of the reasons why John Caig's Sailcraft "Ace 2000" was so popular among the top sailors was because he was the first chandler to add greater control and additional purchase to the basic control lines of the outhaul, kicker and downhaul. Non stretch halyards and a thinner mainsheet on a ratchet block were also beneficial as was a rolled sail.

The next area of concern was the sail, which had a tendency to have a flapping leech on certain points of sailing. A technical committee was formed of Graham Wright and Tim Wills in particular who carried out a series of tests involving the addition of a leech line which if properly adjusted seemed to work and so was added to the Hyde sail. Three fingers of strengthening material were also added to the head and the clew to provide greater strength and stability.

And so it remained for many years but around 2002 the Topper was at a cross roads – sales were steady but pressure was on to order 500 hulls and decks at a time for an economic production run; events were better attended than ever before with 200+ entries now almost guaranteed for both Inland and National Championships; the class itself was in rude health and was poised to see events sailed abroad on a near annual basis (actually it happened in 2004).

But there was suddenly pressure to make changes. In the commercial market the Pico was making inroads especially in the holiday leisure and sailing schools' market and the RYA, having at last decided to include the Topper in its Youth Programme as the boat between the Optimist and the Laser, after neglecting it for so long, were very keen to see it become centre main sheeted in line with other Youth Classes.

Abroad, the aft sheeting system was regarded as old fashioned and was proving increasingly difficult to promote.

The Class Committee discussed the change at length – was this too radical and breaking the original one-design concept; trials were established, conducted by Simon Kearns and the ten best Topper helms of the day, to see if both sheeting methods could compete together on an even playing field; Topper chandlers were quickly ready to provide conversion kits; and finally the Proctor Design Partnership agreed to the change as a way forward, provided that other National Topper Class Associations agreed, and ISAF gave its approval. The standard boat would still be aft-sheeted and the new system would be marketed as a racing option with a longer tiller extension.

Today it is rare to see an aft-sheeted boat at a racing event, though the trials didn't show any benefit in speed – perhaps a more comfortable seating position and certainly a different tacking technique – but at the expense of reducing the room in the cockpit that beach boat users like.

There have been other slight changes that can be made legally. The downhaul has been upgraded from a 3:1 purchase to a 6:1; the centre toe strap can now be any length and can be made adjustable; the halyard has been replaced by a short loop of rope or better still a loop of webbing attached to the sail preventing any stretch; the outhaul cleat on the boom can be changed to a cam cleat; the old rowlock-style gooseneck fitting has been replaced by a better fitting; the kicker take-off points on the mast and boom are now by way of rings and webbing straps; and there is a new stainless steel transom plate to stop slackness. All these modifications have been aimed at greater control and a reduction in breakages as increased loads are applied.

Finally, a new 4.2 sail has been introduced for younger sailors rather than distort a larger sail by constantly reefing and its cut moves the centre of effort to a more effective position.

Like many of these changes this was the brainchild of Dave Cockerill who, working in conjunction with Ian Proctor designs and Topper International, had imported cut down sails for training purposes, proposed an official reduced sail as an option for lighter helms.

These changes throw open the boat to a much wider, smaller, younger group of sailors with an increased attendance at most events with separate fleets, and it has generally brought the age profile of Topper sailors down.

The upshot is that it is much rarer now to see a sailor feature on championship podiums over a period of several years as was the case in the past. The very best – on a roll of success – may win double championships in one year and in exceptional circumstances all three before they move on.

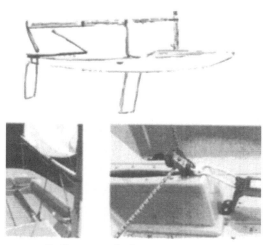

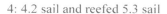

3: Centre mainsheet arrangement

4: 4.2 sail and reefed 5.3 sail

5: ITCA (UK)

A huge part of the success of the Topper dinghy has been the part played by the Committee of the International Topper Class Association (UK) which was formed in 1976. Their brief was to help and promote the sailing of Topper dinghies; to organize two major championships a year – an Inlands on one of the large reservoirs and a National championship to be held on the sea; plus a series of Area and Nationwide championships; to man the stand at the RYA Dinghy Exhibition in March where all classes show off their boats; to produce the Topper Times magazine three times a year and a Year Book in which the fixtures, past results, measurements and constitution are set out. As the Topper is a one design boat the watching brief of the Committee, and the chief Measurer in particular, plays an important policing role in maintaining fair standards of equipment for all and to ensure subsequently fair racing.

The composition of the Committee has not really changed that much over the years – initially there was the designer, Ian Proctor, who was replaced on his death in 1992 by his son, Roger Proctor, as the designer's representative. From the beginning to 2005 there were three Commodores (Geoff Wright, Chris Robinson, Roger Cleland) but the role became superfluous and was subsequently dropped.

There has always been the key figurehead of a Chairman (of which there have been 15); a Vice Chairman (who was fixtures secretary); Treasurer; chief Measurer; representatives from Scotland, Wales, the Midlands, the North West, the North East, the South West, the South East, and the London Area; a Youth/Training Officer and of course the one salaried official, the Secretary (of these there have been 7).

Over the years, as times have changed, new positions have appeared, like International representative, child protection officer, magazine designer and editor (for years it was the Secretary's remit), RYA Topper Coach, chairmen of racing

23

and training, fixtures secretary, RIB master and, since some editions of Topper Times are now produced electronically, a web master for current on-line information.

The modern magazine publication really reflects how things have progressed over the course of time from grainy black and white photographs to outstanding colour action shots and a much more professionally produced magazine, thanks first to a designer plus co-ordinator to a designer plus editor. Although coloured covers appeared from time to time in the early 80s, it wasn't until 2008 that the magazine went all colour.

The format of Topper Times has not changed much over time as it has always included a Chairman's letter, a Secretary's letter, reports on open meetings throughout Great Britain, including strong reports from Northern Ireland and Tartan Toppers, notices of race for all the major National and International championships with full reports and all the results, and advertisements for Insurance, sailing equipment from numerous specialist Topper stockists (Sailcraft's last back cover advert was in 1996 since when several firms have specialised in Topper race kits, trailers, sail tubes etc.) and Topper clothing which was popular before the arrival of squad jackets and polo shirts.

It is difficult to know where to begin to give an impression of all the hundreds of articles that have appeared in Topper Times – there has been such an eclectic mix. There have been letters to the editor in response to previous articles, occasionally to complain, but most often to endorse the sheer fun sailors have experienced with their boat. Early on John Caig had a column with extracts from his book "Topper Sailing" on different controls and techniques and explanations of the mysteries of gate starts. As early as spring 1981 there was a long article on the benefits of having a compass, followed 11 years later by Tony Mountford explaining how to use one at sea to best advantage.

There have been profiles of sailing clubs, committee members and of the most successful winners. Photographs have revealed some strange places to find Toppers and even stranger uses of them, including daft ways of abusing the boat by climbing the mast or seeing how many people you can get on a boat, doing headstands or deliberately pitchpoling. People have written accounts of different exploits and trips or unusual additions like outboard motors and additional sails. There have been personal anecdotes from sailors who have moved on to other classes or from sailors whose perspectives have only ever been from the back of the fleet. Articles have appealed for volunteer committee members where vacancies have unexpectedly occurred. Measurement rules have been explained by chief Measurer, Ian Cox, to leave no doubt about a boat's legality and where in older boats leaks have occurred, there have been numerous suggestions on how to effect repairs, particularly to the transom fittings which in early boats were prone to leak.

Important changes to the boat concerning more powerful controls of the sail and latterly the introduction of the centre main system have been introduced, tested, written about and illustrated as has the introduction of the 4.2 sail. In his capacity as RYA Topper Coach, Dave Cockerill has followed up John Caig's articles with excerpts from his and John's book, "The Topper Book" to maximize sailors' understanding of new developments and techniques in different conditions from hiking out to race strategy, from diet and hydration to fitness.

The structure of the training programme has been explained as it has evolved over the years into today's regional and national squad set-up. There have been periods of introspection when surveys have been carried out and analysed by Colin McNae and Peter Briscall over attendance at open meetings in the different areas in order to give a clear indication as to how well the Topper fleet was holding up.

Amusing articles have appeared, gently poking fun at some of the more eccentric antics of fellow sailors, nostalgic parental reminiscences of their time as drivers, accommodation organisers and general agony aunts/uncles when thing don't go right.

Some articles stand out such as the dramatic beach evacuation by helicopter at North Berwick or the audacious

Channel crossing for charity of two Topper sailors, James Asquith and Jamie Purcell.

We have celebrated not only sailing successes but several weddings (including Bill Brassington's to Cathy Bentley and Adam Cockerill's to Jackie Wilson) and, sadly, funerals. There have also been the RYA Community Awards to Ian Cox, Derek Burchell, Andy Millington, Peter Baldwin and Tim Lowe. HRH the Princess Royal also presented ex-Topper sailors, Craig Paul, Sam Combs and James Hopson with the Raymarine Young Sailor of the Year Award for rescuing a girl crew of a 29er who had been trapped under the boat.

Finally, virtually every edition of the magazine is packed with advice – advice to parents on how to help and what not to do; advice to first time entrants to a major championship; advice on how to rig the boat to meet different wind conditions; advice on suitable clothing for all seasons with accompanying advertisements on how to dress from head to toe, layer upon layer; advice on what to buy to get your boat on the road with sails rolled and all equipment stored on a purpose built trailer – remember car Toppering?

It remains the principal communication vehicle (certainly from an archive perspective) though electronic newsletters have an immediacy that cannot be matched and there is always the official Topper website.

IAN COX has been involved with Toppers for a very long time. He and his late wife, Glynnis, supported their children's Topper careers and in addition he was ITCA Chief Measurer for 14 years. As befits a measurer, he fell easily into the role capitalizing on his natural quiet and calm disposition and innate punctiliousness in ensuring strict adherence to class rules and thereby fair sailing across the fleet.

During his years in office, he oversaw the huge development of the centre-main sheeting system to the point where there are virtually no aft-sheeted Toppers in the racing fleets of today.

When he retired as ITCA GBR Chief Measurer, he became measurer and technical representative to the International Committee and is now a recognized ISAF Measurer. His dedication and hard work over the years were recognized in 2008 when he received a Community Award from the RYA, presented to him by HRH the Princess Royal in London.

HELEN EVANS was the Class Secretary for 23 years and even when she retired from that position, she still maintained her links by continuing as International Secretary. She had been a school secretary but a chance advert in Yachts and Yachting in 1982 caught her eye and tempted her to make a career change.

After some hesitation and self doubt she accepted the post which turned out to be more a way of life than a job. Fortunately the Evans family were already used to sailing but becoming the Class Secretary proved to be a sharp learning curve with all the many aspects of dealing with boat insurance, committee meetings, manning the Dinghy Show stand, enquiries at all times of the day and night, publicity, the editing of Topper Times and banking all falling under her remit.

Her skills and efficiency became taken for granted – even the transition to computers was taken in her stride. Ably assisted by her husband, Alan, she was always there for everybody and was so well loved and respected by all age groups that she has attended Topper sailors' weddings and even sadly funerals. Even through some difficult times she came through smiling and on retirement thanked all the many officials and sailors alike who helped along the way.

Geoff Wright
1973-1984

Chris Robinson
1984-1987

Graham Wright
1987-1990

Hilary Talbot
1990-1993

Alex Bailey
1993-1995

Roger Cleland
1995-1999

David Garth
1999-2000

Nick Skinner
2000-2002

John Smalley
2002-2005

5: Past Chairmen to 2005

Miles Palmer
2005-2008

Charles Glover
2008-2010

Jonathan Cunnison
2010-2012

Tom Dixon
2012-2013

Adam McElroy
2013-2014

Sally Dugdale
2014-

6: Past Chairmen from 2005

| Ron Hope | Wendy Fitzpatrick | Vicki Watson |
| 1973-1976 | 1976-1979 | 1979-1981 |

| Kathy Price | Helen Evans | Susan Wellerd |
| 1981-1982 | 1982-2005 | 2005-2014 |

Jeanette Sanderson
2014-

7: Past Secretaries

8: Unusual uses of the Topper
Clockwise from top left: Tony Bedwell; O level revision 1986; Priestley's idea; tender in Hong Kong; German garden; Down Under. *Centre* Joe Smith on his way to Loch Tay 1986

9: Topper Times covers

30th July - 5th August

10: Yearbooks and Handbooks

11: The cover of the original Dunhill Manual

6: TRAINING

For many years the Topper was regarded by the more established sailing community and the RYA as a fun boat – not to be taken seriously, despite the RYA's National Sailing Coach, John Driscoll's report in 1984 extolling the virtues of the Topper for training purposes. It was if you like the ugly duckling of the junior racing classes. But like the ugly duckling it began to grow and it became increasingly obvious that the Topper was not a duck after all. The large numbers at the Women's Nationals and the NSSA Regattas, where classes were mixed, proved that here was a much bigger bird – perhaps a swan. To reinforce the point, Hilary Talbot as Chairman at the time wrote on more than one occasion to the RYA to complain about the way Toppers were treated at the Women's Nationals. One such letter to John Derbyshire was endorsed by Tony Mountford who watched the Toppers race alongside the new ladies Olympic boat, the Europe, in 1989. He wrote "if handicap had been taken into consideration I think all the Toppers would have beaten all the Europes.... the RYA had better wake up to the fact that if they are looking for future champions they should spend more time looking at real talent in the Toppers and less time watching expensive Olympic boats".

Co-incidentally at this time some youth classes, particularly Cadets, were beginning to struggle with numbers. Slowly, slowly the RYA began to take more of an interest – they appointed coaches to boost the in–house training and in 1998 Jim Saltonstall paid a visit to the Nationals at Feltham. Eventually, the Topper was added to the RYA "Pathway" list of boats for the progression of young sailors up the Olympic pyramid. As Danny Kaye would have observed –"a very fine swan indeed".

Topper training began from quite humble beginnings as local clubs put on sessions for their own youngsters to introduce them into racing. The first Training Officer on the

TICA Committee was John Myles, a London-based coach, who was soon followed in 1988 by the appointment of Tony Mountford from Chelmarsh SC as the RYA National Coach. Prior to that it had been possible for some of the best helms to attend a Jim Saltonstall run RYA weekend for all youth classes without separate coaching for Toppers. For the first time and almost single-handedly, Tony brought in a more structured and professional approach to training. In recognition of his work, the RYA in conjunction with the Eric Twiname Trust provided the class with its own support boat, Eric Twiname III, to bring it into line with the Optimist, 420 and Laser classes. He wrote articles in Topper Times on the necessity to train not only on the water but also to improve their physical fitness. At his sailing camps, often in the winter months, he ran early morning PE sessions, briefings on sailing in different conditions, exercises in starting, mark rounding tacking and gybing and sailing within the laylines.

Over seven years he and Derek Burchell from Broxbourne SC, often working in tandem as well as separately, transformed a previous ad hoc arrangement into a formal system of squads for U16 males, youth males U19 and a female squad. Acknowledging that many adults also sailed Toppers, he tried on several occasions to arrange adult training but was foiled in this through lack of support. The squads were known as the 'Topper National Squad' which were trained both as individual squads but also as a group. Those that were most successful gained places on John Swannie's 'High Flyers' courses though he always offered "wild cards" to others who had not qualified but who he regarded as potential champions. His background was in wider RYA Training both at home and abroad and his style was less dogmatic than many. He had a charisma in getting the best out of his charges and often half joked about achieving the 'Northern Dream' of a northern nationals winner which Stephen Cleland realised at Filey in 1992.

Unfortunately the inevitable clash of coaching styles led partly to the demise of both coaches within the Topper scene – John's involvement tailed off and Tony felt that he no longer had the backing of the committee. This resulted in a number of others, Derek Burchell, Richard Linsdale and Margaret Delaney forming a Training Sub-Committee which maintained the training programmes until Chris Gowers, Mark Baron, Tim Hall (Wales), had brief spells as principal coaches. In the end it was felt that a more mature figure should be the RYA Topper Coach and Dave Cockerill was appointed – a position he held for 14 years

During this period of flux the one constant factor was the continuity provided by Nick Skinner who took over the Youth Squad and Derek Burchell who, as acting RYA National Coach, continued the training, holding training camps and arranging local training to be offered around the country. Even when a new RYA Topper Coach was appointed, the latter continued to play an important supporting role using the Bradwell Centre in Essex.

The Cockerill years saw many changes not just in training which always had to be fun but in changes to the boat, all aimed at making it more of a racing machine of a more controllable nature and with an easier hiking position. The introduction of the 4.2 rig opened up the boat to a younger, lighter and less experienced group of youngsters.

Judging from the most recent Topper Times the selection and training of the different squads dominate the calendar and yet letters re-inforce the pleasure gained from such sessions (phrases like "the journey home was a continuous account of things learned and the fun that had been had") was typical. Clearly the RYA, having selected the Topper as a "pathway" boat on the progression upwards towards Olympic boats was keen to see the age profile come down and fit in more closely with what they saw as the natural progression up the triangle. So time spent in Toppers for many is often less than four years.

The resulting squads took on a pyramid of their own – at the top was a National Junior Squad (24 u15 sailors); a National Intermediate Squad (24u15 sailors); RYA Zone Squads (24u14 sailors); ITCA GBR Squad; ITCA 4.2 Squad and local clubs training; ITCA Racing Squad (26 u14 sailors not selected elsewhere) and a Youth Squad (32 u18 sailors too old for other training). These squads have been coached by a number of different coaches – RYA High Performance Managers often took on Regional Zone Squads; the Intermediate Squad was coached by Adam Cockerill and the Junior Squad by Dave Cockerill (he also ran the 4.2 Squad sponsored by Sailing Solutions and later the All Girls Squad.) The ITCA GBR Youth Squad was coached by Ian Patience followed by Niall Myant and the Junior Development Squad by Nathan Batchelor – both these sponsored by Purple Marine. Other coaches are brought in from time to time to help out at varying levels and parental volunteers are an added bonus. In 2015 Natalie Wood was appointed RYA Head Topper Coach.

As you can imagine competition for places is very fierce and there are many disappointed sailors, but when you consider the amount of weekend winter training, a spring camp and pre Nationals and pre Worlds training for the best, it is not surprising.

With all this emphasis on age and recommended weight you do just pause and reflect. Does this mean that sailors like the late Catrina Drummond and Rebecca Hulse and the very senior and ever cheerful Bill Catt, who so enjoyed their sailing and participation in a big event, have been or are being edged out of the Nationals and Inlands scene? I hope not. I hope that an adult sailor in the mould of a Tim Wills will appear in order to set a bench mark against whom fast moving transitional sailors can really be compared and thereby give real perspective. I hope too that parents may feel, where circumstances allow, that they compete alongside or more likely behind their offsprings in order to experience the same highs and lows that competition brings.

There is no doubt that it is a major part of the RYA's remit to pursue ever-increasing standards in order to deliver Olympians and world champions for team GBR. These standards have undoubtedly increased enormously and are often seen as worthy in themselves, and have had a major impact on the Topper. For some it promotes the dream of sailing stardom in much the same way as professional football clubs. However we should also always ask the question, if not undertaken in a balanced way, does it also harbour the danger of leaving behind some disappointed youngsters who may take a long time to find their spiritual home in other classes, if not in Toppers?

Therefore it perhaps is a question we should be prepared to revisit and debate on a regular basis. It will always be a balance between the need to win and also discovering and nurturing a lifelong love of sailing for fun and local competition. The Topper is known as 'the friendly class' and should aspire to remain so. So if we continue to examine this question, it is my belief the Topper will always strike the right balance for all sailors of all abilities, now and in the future.

DAVE COCKERILL's background to sailing was in Cadets and Graduates, then a Europe and finally in Buzzes and Isos. He was introduced to Toppers by his son, Adam, whilst professionally he started out as a Technology teacher before owning the chandlery, Sailing Solutions, and embarking on his career as a coach. His contribution to the ongoing development of the Topper has been immense. Not only has he coached literally hundreds of sailors as the Head Coach of the RYA Topper (GBR) Squad over his 14 year tenure (which in 2005 was recognised by the award of RYA Squad Coach of the Year), but at a time when the Topper was under pressure commercially, he introduced a number of changes to the boat. Working closely with the Proctor Design Partnership and Topper International, these changes have enabled the boat to fit in more closely with the RYA Pathway scheme and to be more attractive to the all-important overseas market.

His first innovation was the introduction of the centre main sheeting arrangement which made for a better hiking position. Another brain child was the introduction of the 4.2 sail, deriving from his own cut down version of the original 5.3 rig, which opened up the boat to a younger, lighter group of sailors and the more powerful controls of a 6:1 downhaul, stronger gooseneck, adjustable toe strap and longer tiller extension made for a more controllable rig. Further work on the sail and its provider made them more affordable and saw the 4.2 being adopted as a sub-class in its own right, for which he was National Coach for five years.

He coached the all-girls National Squad which in 2015 produced the first female National champion since 1976.

12: Chelmarsh 1992 and Tony Mountford

13: John Reed (right) of the Eric Twiname Trust handing over the Tornado support boat to Tony Mountford. Jim Saltonstall admires the boat.

14: High Flyers and John Swannie 1993

15: All-Girl Squad and Dave Cockerill

16: National Youth Squad and Ian Patience

17: Bradwell Centre and Derek Burchell

43

18: 4.2 Squad 2012

19: National Youth Squad 2012

7: RACING

Racing has always been at the forefront of the Class Association from the early days of one of the Proctor sons and David Hoskins both buying fibreglass Toppers to join in the racing with six other boats at Linlithgow Loch SC during their summer holidays.

During the late 70s, 80s and early 90s, as racing became more and more established from club racing, often in mixed handicap fleets, to clubs holding specific Topper open meetings, there was always a group of good adult sailors (John Caig, Dave Parkinson, Graham Wright, Mike Holmes, Martin Treadway, Giles Trollope, Jon Franklin, Tony Prangnell, Janet Thompson, Margaret Delaney, Debbie Degge, Barry White, Perri Cannon, Owen Clarkson Primrose Salt – to name a few) who regularly met at the bigger events and against whom up-and-coming juniors aspired to and sometimes did beat. Add to this mix ex juniors/young adults who, having left the class, were often tempted to have a go at a major championship if they could get hold of a competitive boat. Allied to this was a posse of parents also competing so in total there was a combination of mixed age range sailing of a unique blend which other classes did not have.

Two sailors from this era stand out for their consistency and frequent successes; firstly John Caig (aka Mr Topper) and later Tim Wills who took over his mantle as always being in the running for a podium place at major events.

But the Class has moved on. Numbers participating at major championships, whilst declining in some long established classes, continued to grow and when entries reached into over 200 it was sensibly decided to move away from one huge gate start to dividing the fleet into three flights of gold, silver and bronze (which first occurred at Downs SC in 2002). This resulted in two outcomes – it gave a wider range of ability of sailor the opportunity to compete for prizes in a way that a single fleet never could and it heralded a huge shift in the overall age profile of competitors.

The Trophies awarded at the Nationals and Inland championships have over the years changed too. The original ones were awarded for the individual races of the large fleet which sailed one long race a day, followed by some overall prizes. The modern fleets, sailing several races a day, now have re-allocated original trophies and added many more, reflecting the different age ranges and sail configurations (see Appendix on Original One Fleet Start Trophies).

One trophy has been constant throughout and that is the Nationwide trophy which is awarded to the sailor who has competed in five events in three different regions and amassed the highest number of points on the basis of 50 points for a win plus the number of boats beaten. The consistent, well- travelled sailor comes out on top.

As the backbone of the Class, Topper sailors have come from many and varied local clubs – some, because of their size, offer only local club racing; others host open meetings and area championships and the lottery of where you live determines the kind of water that you grow up with. Some sailors are lucky – their home clubs are situated on some of the largest reservoirs in the country (Grafham Water, Rutland Water, Draycote Water, Chew Valley Lake, Kielder Water, Llyn Brenig, Queen Mary Reservoir and Carsington Water); others are on the majestic lakes, lochs and loughs of the United Kingdom (Ullswater, Loch Lomond, Lough Neagh); some are hidden away in desolate areas like the former Llyn Aled SC in the Denbighshire hills; and some are on rivers and creeks where the decision to tack can be as much influenced by wishing to avoid a clash with a rowing eight as by any wind shift; some are in coastal venues boasting the title of "Royal" with splendid club houses very much in keeping with their status. All are cherished as "home waters" providing venues as diverse as they are too numerous to mention and yet which from time to time produce sailors of outstanding ability.

Wherever racing has taken place, and especially at big events, it has been fair, enjoyable and highly competitive.

Sadly, I recall one bad exception in the mid 90s when an experienced adult sailor who was very much in contention to win overall was effectively ganged up on through nods and winks by a group of junior sailors who sailed him down the fleet. Thankfully, in 14 years experience of Nationals, this was very much the exception and was a lesson to all concerned about sportsmanship. At the other end of the fleet where little wind and strong tides have tested the judgement of a whole host of sailors, the resulting collisions and rafting up at a mark have brought forward no protests nor exonerating penalties. Again, lessons do get learned if only seeing more lowly placed competitors sail round the obstruction and profit from the mayhem. It is all part of the individual learning curve of racing management in different conditions and on different waters.

From time to time, a few competitors have triumphed by winning two National titles, or a Nationals and a Worlds or an Inland championship followed in the same year with a win in the Nationals or the Worlds. But it has been surprisingly rare and healthily reflects just how strongly competitive Topper racing is. As young sailors quickly move on up and into other boats, encouraged by the RYA pyramid system of searching for future Olympic champions, it becomes less likely to occur. Sometimes sailors who have been very successful return to compete in a Nationals or a Worlds (as I mentioned earlier) with often, to some people, surprising success. The reality is that these sailors, like the older adult winners of yesteryear, have learned how to race, how to manage the pressures of a championship week and most importantly how to win.

However, there have been numerous articles, admittedly by some of the older sailors, who have questioned from time to time whether racing is the only pleasure to be had from a Topper. In the mid 90s Roger Proctor wrote a long article of its time in Topper Times in which he questioned whether to race or not and which, with his permission, I reproduce here.

"Over the last few years it has become apparent to me that Topper sailors are a pretty broad bunch. This follows the research that has been done by the Class Association, talking to the members I meet, and also through the conversations I have had with International members, such as those in Germany. The group that is the most committed to organizing events, vocal and willing to give up their time, are the racing fraternity. Indeed it is true to say that the main bulk of the Class Committee is made up of members who either themselves or their children race consistently. These committee members are a dedicated and hard-working team who selflessly give up much of their free time for the benefit of the Class Association.

I have become worried that over the last few years the membership numbers seem stuck at around 1,800. Bearing in mind that nearly 900 new boats are sold yearly, each of which comes with a free membership, and that there are 36,000 boats throughout the world, it is a worry that we only seem to have a renewing membership of around 1,000. Why is this?

Naturally there will be a fallout of new members. People lose interest, gain different interests, forget to pay, whatever. However, I am concerned that it may also be because they do not find the interest and benefit that they seek from being a member of the Class Association.

People who buy Toppers may do so for very different reasons. Yes, many people do race, are dedicated to it or do it purely for fun. However, there are I believe many other types of sailors. For example, people who buy a boat just so they can have it on the beach during their holiday and do a bit of fun sailing. People who sail with friends and use it socially. People who are learning to sail. The reasons are many and varied. But what is clear to me is that there is a significant non-racing community. I believe it is our duty as a Class Association to appeal to these sections. It is our job to represent the views and wishes of all Topper sailors. We should encourage membership and increase it. By increasing membership we can do more.

There was and is a vision for the Topper. It was designed as a cheap sailing boat that is fun to sail with a primary purpose of introducing as many people as possible to the joys of sailing. It was also to be used as a strictly one design racing boat, but not exclusively so. The Class Association was set up to create a family of members who could learn from each other, share their sailing experiences and become a Topper community. With the introduction of International status we now have an opportunity to build a world-wide Topper family.

I have had several discussions with some of the Germans and they have a different view of the Topper than many UK members. For them it is a much more of a social boat.

They have sailing weekends away and go cruising. They feel the UK is very competitive and only about racing. I do not believe that actually this is the case but it is the face of the Class Association that is currently projected through its fixture lists and magazines.

.....

I know the Topper is not a cruising boat and this is not the essence of my argument. That much I hope is obvious. We must accept that the boat is used in many different ways. What we need to do is to create a body of volunteers within the Class Association who are prepared to take on the interests of the non-racing members, develop programmes for them and so broaden the appeal of being a Topper Class Association member.

.....

I do urge you to think creatively, think about how you sail the boat and what you enjoy doing. Perhaps you race already, but maybe you also use the boat purely for the sheer joy of sailing, for holidays, for cruising, exploring etc.. Tell us what you do and share it with everyone.

.....

These may all be badly thought out, simplistic and ill conceived ideas but whatever they are, I need to know whether anyone agrees with my views. Your thoughts would therefore be greatly appreciated. In conclusion, the Topper is undoubtedly a wonderful boat. It gives people the opportunity to enjoy sailing in so many ways. We need to represent those various ways of using the boat in the way the Class Association organizes itself and your help is required to make this happen."

As you would expect there were lots of replies. Some from dedicated racers simply didn't have the time or the inclination to do anything but race. Yet a good number were in support of his thesis, but only on an individual basis with no grand mass explorations, including from an ex-windsurfer, a 14 stone man and a 46 year old midwife who obtained great pleasure in sailing single-handed in Poole and Brittany. How many more of us have taken a Topper on holiday here or abroad and sailed off the beach just for fun? About the same time Hilary Talbot wrote a long article about a holiday on the Norfolk Broads on a cruiser but with two Toppers in tow for her and Graham Wright. Citing "Swallows and Amazons" as a model they crossed the major lakes and tacked up narrow waterways and even under the odd bridge by dropping the mast at the last moment. And very much in the German style of social cruising with BBQs and sing songs, I suspect that there are local authority outdoor education centres and commercial leisure sailing companies at home and abroad who organize similar expeditions for their clients. Even here though, the temptation to see whether you can make your boat go faster than the next one prompts a sense of racing to dominate. For sailing clubs it is their "raison d'être" and for the Class Association, it is what they support and promote very successfully.

To close this section on racing it is worth reflecting on sponsorship, which, like so much of what has happened with Toppers, has grown and grown over the years. In the early years, local firms and chandlers might offer some sponsorship for a large event but more often than not there is a reliance on the generosity of Topper International to supply a boat or a sail to be auctioned or as a prize for a Travellers series. Occasionally, a Topper stockist would institute their own regional Travellers/Knockout series with some very generous prizes, from a new boat in exchange for a second-hand one, to clothing and an assortment of sailing "goodies". In the latest years, sponsorship has become much more keenly sought after and more prominently and professionally displayed – most major events now attract multiple sponsors of either international, national or local standing (or all three).

Contrary to what many purists believed (there were fears that boats and sails would look like Formula One racing cars covered in adverts), it has not tainted the sport but rather enabled events to be financially secure and more professionally run which, in view of the numbers involved, has become a necessity. That these companies wish to be associated with the Class is a reflection on the kudos that the boat has earned.

Today's competitors don't just receive a notice of race but a comprehensive handbook covering every possible aspect of the racing, facilities on offer and area information. Such publications are not cheap to produce.

You may wonder what has become of the best Topper helms over the years. Some have gone on to succeed in other classes – certainly in the Youth Classes where they have acquitted themselves well in National Youth Squads at ISAF World Youth Events. A few have gone on to be on the fringe of Olympic selection, some have actually made the GBR team and shown great spirit and one, Helena Lucas, has actually proved Tony Mountford prescient when he wrote in Spring 1992.... "one day an Olympic gold medalist is going to be an ex Topper helm". She won gold in 2012 in a 2.4 paralympic keelboat. With fingers crossed, we await to see if Giles Scott and others can repeat the feat in 2016. We hope so. As for the many, many others, most have grown up, moved on, married and have young children who may yet start the whole thing all over again some day hence.

JOHN CAIG was for many years "Mr Topper". He had already had a distinguished sailing career being twice Fireball European Champion and a member of the British Olympic Sailing team in 1972 before committing himself wholeheartedly to Topper sailing. His list of successes are legendary with World titles in 1979 and 1985 and a second in 1981; National titles in 1980, l982, 1983, 1984 with a third place in 1981; and Inland titles in 1984, 1985 and 1990 with a third place in 1988.

In the 1980s, he was the man to beat and yet he was always modest in victory and defeat alike, often encouraging young aspiring sailors. His book, "Topper Sailing" was published in 1982 and has since been updated in collaboration with RYA Topper Coach, Dave Cockerill. Aspects of his technique on different points of sailing were often reprinted in Topper Times for the benefit of up-and-coming sailors, as has the later version.

His business, John Caig Sailcraft, of selling his racing version of a Topper with better and more adjustable fittings and a rolled sail, with its distinctive bottom light blue panel and non-digital numbers, became the sought-after boat of its day and a forerunner of many race prepared boats on today's market.

TIM WILLS took over from John Caig in the 1990s as the most successful and consistent Topper sailor, although despite a World title in 1992 and four Inland Championships he never managed to win a National title, coming second in 1993, 1995 and 1997 and third in 1991 and 1998. His sailing background was very broad and extensive from Cadets, Mirrors, Merlin Rockets, 505s and Flying Fifteens and with National titles in a Pandora in 1980 and a Marauder in 1985.

A back injury and a long lay-off from sailing preceded his Topper career which was originally to assist his recuperation but which proved to be so enjoyable that he stuck with Toppers as his main boat. Open meetings and the World Championship in Finland, where he gained a second place, confirmed his decision.

Tim has been an excellent role model, always competitive but generous in his encouragement to younger sailors. His brief spell on the Topper Committee was put to good use, in conjunction with Graham Wright, in testing the flapping leeches of early sails before leech lines were introduced. Sadly, such "older" characters no longer exist in the modern Topper fleet, which is a pity because you could always guarantee that he would give any youngster a good race.

8: THE FRIENDLY CLASS

On the Topper website it states that…. "ITCA (GBR) is the Class Association for Topper Sailors in the UK. We are known as "The Friendly Class" with sailors keen to welcome new members and parents and supporters who are always happy to help one another and promote good sportsmanship.

We organize coaching and racing events for Topper sailors both at a regional level and nationally, and although the Topper is sailed predominately by junior sailors we have active members of all ages in our fleet".

What makes it known as the "Friendly Class"? Is such an expression saying something about other classes? It's certainly an expression that's been around for a long time, so what's the explanation?

Historically, it's been a class that embraced all ages, juniors, adults and seniors (or veterans as they were once called) and allowed both sexes equal opportunities to do well. You will recall from Ian Proctor's articles that these criteria were very much in the forefront of his original thinking and were borne out by the early successes of 60 year old Bridget Quick and Wendy Fitzpatrick. Secondly, there was for a very long time a group of adult sailors who were not only very good role models but whom juniors, given the right conditions, could sometimes beat. Far from creating resentment, the older sailors encouraged and celebrated their young rivals' success.

Junior sailors are often at an age when they rely totally on parents for transport and organizing accommodation but who very often begin to take ownership of the rigging and de-rigging of their boat (it becomes a matter of pride for some) and certainly sail their own races, making their own decisions and not as the frustrated extension of non-participating parents. The most helpful and constructive advice comes from coaches.

The fierce rivalry on the water paradoxically was closely linked to the strong friendships among competitors who used to phone one another to check which events were being attended, not so as to avoid each other but to meet up with friends. The very fact that races had a blend of different aged competitors also added a calming influence on some of the wilder excesses that over-keen sailors might try on by flouting the rules either knowingly or through ignorance. The result was sportsmanship was the winner to everyone's benefit. And there has always been a lot of respect shown by competitors to their fellow competitors of all ages, and by parents and supporters of the sailors involved.

Much of this enjoyment has been reflected in articles in Topper Times over the years – nostalgic reminiscences of different venues, new friends that have become old friends among all ages, and a certain sadness that the inevitable moving on to Lasers, Laser Radials, 420s or 29ers means the end of an era. I would imagine that such friendliness is carried forward into the next class chosen though whether the same chemistry of all aspects of Topper racing exists will vary from person to person and from class to class.

Other wise opinion has suggested that the boat is almost unique in that you can't throw money at it in order to buy success (another of the designer's ideas). The nature of the rig of the Topper means that controls can be adjusted on the water (increasingly so over the years with more powerful fittings) rather than rely on a parent to set the boat up for you before a race and the sails are all the same for everyone. As Dave Cockerill wrote in Topper Times in the summer of 2006… " the Topper is fun to sail but that does not account for why the people associated with the Topper are such fun to be around. The sailors, young and not so young, always look happy on the water… it's the same story on the shore. Certainly the helpers are keen to see their charges do well but I don't see the tense, grumpy faces around that I hear about in other classes." He speaks of the willingness to help to launch boats, sort out breakages (even other people's), man support boats and generally offer to help.

I recall, as Chairman, vacancies in the post of Area Representative never being a problem for long as someone always stepped up and gave invaluable service to the class. Such support on and off the water must be the envy of lots of classes.

During the course of this history the blend of different aged sailors has been a key feature but the vexed question arises as to when the time comes to move on to another (nowadays) "pathway" class or not. Twenty years ago, sailors of about 16 or 17 moved up often to the Laser class when they could manage the bigger rig and compete for Youth Squad places. Increasingly, in recent times with pyramids and the proliferation of Topper squads, the pressure from the RYA to move on and leave Toppers behind is very strong, but there must be lots of able sailors, perhaps not in the top flight, who would be far happier staying where they are and enjoying all that Toppers have to offer. There might also be financial and logistical problems, particularly where a two-man boat is concerned, to say nothing of the external pressure of schooling and exams.

Lastly, for many years, particularly through the 80s and 90s, there was always a strong social programme at National Championships which brought everyone together. Discos and ceilidhs were popular before a time when each individual had his or her own music station via a phone or an iplayer and games nights saw teams of all ages taking part and letting their hair down. It all added to the cohesion of the class.

20: World Championship, Workum 2012 (unknown)

21: National Championship, Paignton 2008 (Peter Norman)

22: Nationals venues. Circle size indicates how often held there

9: CONCLUSION

My wife and I, like so many groups of parents up and down the land, look back with great pleasure and thankfulness at our "Topper years". Weekends saw homework being dashed off on a Friday evening to leave Saturday and Sunday free to attend open meetings or area championships all over the country and a chance to meet up with like-minded friends (parents and offsprings) and yet great rivals on the water.

You read so often of young people who have become couch potatoes, who through boredom become a nuisance element to society and who have lost their way in the education system. Are these the same young people who sail regularly – I don't think so. The dedication demanded of them is such that there is no room for such idleness.

Walk round any championship dinghy park and you can't fail to be caught up in the buzz of boat preparation, of clusters of friends proudly sporting their squad jackets or other regalia while others look on, enviously aspiring to join them at some future date. Their commitment to the sport is admirable and all consuming; their parents' support is invaluable and yet so often silently taken for granted.

But spare a thought for a moment for all those hundreds of ordinary club sailors and leisure sailors who happily enjoy their sailing, whether on a small scale competitively or even just for fun, for whom squads and podium finishes are from a different world.

The sum of the whole leaves one with a sense of optimism for the future and long may that continue.

I started this history, more or less, with words written by Ian Proctor and so it is perhaps fitting that I should end with some words that he wrote in the 1983 summer edition of Topper Times.

"As the class grows from strength to strength and there are more and more Topper helmsmen competing for the racing honours, let us never allow the mere size of the class or keenness of competition endanger the friendliness and fun.... Of course the competition should be keen and skillful, but let us always try to ensure that the spirit of the Topper class and its sense of sportsmanship and enjoyment remains our prime objective. That is an asset that many other classes have lost as they grew bigger – and we know that the decline in dinghy racing in general in the past few years is partly due to that. If we build on our present reputation for having that priceless asset, we can't go wrong."

Amen to that.

APPENDICES

MULTIPLE WINNERS

TWO NATIONAL CHAMPIONSHIPS		

John Caig 1980, 82,83,84	Tony Prangnell 1985,1990	Stephen Cleland 1992, 93

Michael Gatward 1997,98	Bleddyn Mon 2005,06	Giles Kuzyk 2011,12
NATIONALS AND INLANDS (in same year)		
John Caig 1984		Tony Prangnell 1985

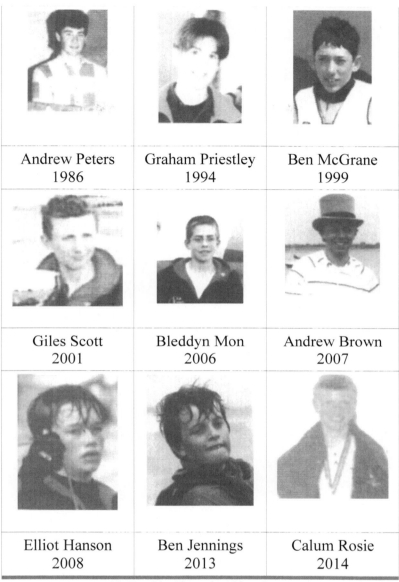

Andrew Peters 1986	Graham Priestley 1994	Ben McGrane 1999
Giles Scott 2001	Bleddyn Mon 2006	Andrew Brown 2007
Elliot Hanson 2008	Ben Jennings 2013	Calum Rosie 2014

23: Double Championship winners

	**WORLDS AND INLANDS** Campbell Davidson 2003
	**TWO WORLDS** Ian Fryett 1982 & 1984
	NATIONALS, WORLDS & INLANDS IN SAME YEAR
	Andrew Peters 1986
	Bleddyn Mon 2005
	Elliot Hanson 2008
	Giles Kuzyk 2012

24: Double and Triple winners

NATIONAL CHAMPIONSHIP WINNERS

1973   Langstone Harbour   10 entries
1st   Roger Proctor
2nd Brian Proctor

1974   Bosham SC
1st   Ron Hope

1975   Bosham SC
1st   Bridget Quick

1976   Bosham SC   30 entries
1st   Wendy Fitzpatrick

1977
1st   Bill Woodhouse

1978   Pagham SC   104 entries
1st   Mike Budd   Lowton SC
2nd Stephen Copley   Lowton SC
3rd Gerry Philbrick   PooleYC

1979   Grafham Water SC
1st   John Ball   Beauchamp Lodge SC
2nd Peter Stratton   Weir Wood SC
3rd John Caig   Poole YC

1980   Paignton SC   154 entries
1st   John Caig   Walton on Thames SC
2nd Chris Jones   Chew Valley Lake SC
3rd Graham Wright   Wisbech YC

1981 Porthpean SC   140 entries
1st Ian Fryett   Chew Valley Lake SC
2nd Ian Wright   Greenlands Dock SC
3rd John Caig   Walton on Thames SC

1982 Holyhead SC   103 entries
1st John Caig   Walton on Thames SC
2nd Jason Hughes   Draycote SC
3rd Ian Fryett   Chew Valley Lake SC

1983 Kessingland SC   100 entries
1st John Caig   Walton on Thames SC
2nd Ian Fryett   Chew Valley Lake SC
3rd Jon Franklin   Maidenhead SC

1984 Abersoch YC   140 entries
1st John Caig   Walton on Thames SC
2nd Philip Allen   Walton on Thames SC
3rd Huw Ragatt   Emberton Park SC

1985 Felpham SC   140 entries
1st Tony Prangnell   Hunts SC
2nd Andrew Peters   Bowmoor SC
3rd Andrew Rice   Walton on Thames SC

1986 Penzance SC   101 entries
1st Andrew Peters   Bowmoor SC
2nd Ashley Taylor   Christchurch SC
3rd Andrew Carter   Herne Bay SC

1987   Thorpe Bay SC   117 entries
1st   Andrew Norman   Scaling Dam SC
2nd Andrew Carter   Herne Bay SC
3rd   Debbie Degge   Sandwell Valley SC

1988   Tenby SC   125 entries
1st   Brian Worrall   Bowmoor SC
2nd Steven Carr   Stokes Bay SC
3rd   Tony Prangnell   Hunts SC

1989   East Lothian YC   102 entries
1st   Jeremy Styles   Downs SC
2nd Andrew Carter   Herne Bay SC
3rd   Chris Reynolds   Locks SC

1990   Mayflower SC Plymouth   128 entries
1st   Tony Prangnell   Hunts SC
2nd Andrew Carter   Herne Bay SC
3rd   Kevin Norton   Papercourt SC

1991   Llandudno SC   130 entries
1st   Gordon Miller   Rutland SC
2nd Graham Priestley   Ullswater YC
3rd   Tim Wills   Grafham Water SC

1992   Filey SC   130 entries
1st   Stephen Cleland   Nelson Centre SC
2nd Gordon Miller   Rutland SC
3rd   Grant Munro   Ullswater YC

1993 Felpham SC   162 entries
1st Stephen Cleland Nelson Centre SC
2nd Tim Wills Grafham Water SC
3rd Graham Priestley Ullswater YC

1994 Royal Torbay YC 150 entries
1st Graham Priestley Ullswater YC
2nd Anthony Edwards Bath University SC
3rd Mark Styles Downs SC

1995 East Lothian YC 121 entries
1st Justin Deal Chew Valley Lake SC
2nd Tim Wills Grafham Water SC
3rd John Burchell Broxbourne SC

1996 Downs SC   136 entries
1st Andrew Palmer-Felgate Spinnaker SC
2nd Stephen Cleland Nelson Centre SC
3rd Jerry Styles Downs SC

1997 Llandudno SC 161 entries
1st Michael Gatward Melton Mowbray SC
2nd Tim Wills Grafham Water SC
3rd Susan Ogg Redditch SC

1998 Felpham SC   137 entries
1st Michael Gatward Melton Mowbray SC
2nd Anthony Bates Ullswater YC
3rd Tim Wills Grafham Water SC

1999	Paignton SC	167 entries
1st	Ben McGrane	Chew Valley Lake SC
2nd	Andy Gatward	Melton Mowbray SC
3rd	Chris Graham	Jebel Ali SC UAE

2000	East Lothian YC	120 entries
1st	Andrew Brooks	Elton SC
2nd	Richard Peacock	Redditch SC
3rd	Chris Catt	Downs SC

2001	Pwllheli SC	187 entries
1st	Giles Scott	Grafham Water SC
2nd	Mark Heather	Wilsonian SC
3rd	Adam Cockerill	Ely SC

2002	Downs SC	216 entries
1st	Simon Kearns	Grafham Water SC
2nd	Steve Jackson	Hardway SC
3rd	Chris Catt	Downs SC

2003	Sunderland SC	229 entries
1st	Richard Valentine	Great Moor SC
2nd	Nathan Batchelor	Clevedon SC
3rd	William Espiner	Great Moor SC

2004	Plymouth SC	246 entries
1st	Rob Partridge	Budworth SC
2nd	Adam Fox	Stewartby SC
3rd	Craig Paul	Lochaber SC

2005   Largs   279 entries
1st Bleddyn Mon   Red Wharf Bay SC
2nd Oscar McVeigh   Wimbledon Park SC
3rd Peter Irwin   Linlithgow Loch SC

2006   Weymouth   289 entries
1st Bleddyn Mon   Red Wharf Bay SC
2nd Andrew Brown   Budworth SC
3rd Thomas Gillard   Rotherham SC

2007   East Lothian YC   289 entries
1st Andrew Brown   Budworth SC
2nd Stephen Beckett   SolvaRowing&W'sports
3rd Jack Hopkins   Delph SC

2008   Paignton SC   276 entries
1st Elliot Hanson   Redesmere SC
2nd Felicity Foulds   Norfolk Broads YC
3rd Lorenzo Chiavarini   Royal Northern Clyde

2009   Pwllheli SC   302 entries
1st Christopher Eames   Strangford Lough YC
2nd Oliver Wright   Rotherham SC
3rd Felicity Foulds   Norfolk Broads YC

2010   Pwllheli SC   323 entries
1st Finn Lynch   Blessington SC
2nd Edward Jones   Chew Valley Lake SC
3rd George Meredith   Grafham Water SC

2011   East Lothian YC   274 entries

1st	Giles Kuzyk	Parkstone YC
2nd	Matt Venables	Sutton SC
3rd	Curtis Mearns	Leigh & Lowton SC

2012		Pwllheli SC	265 entries
1st	Giles Kuzyk	Parkstone YC	
2nd	Ross McFarlane	Castle Cove SC	
3rd	Lawrence Logan	Nott'shire Co. SC	

2013		Weymouth	250 entries
1st	Ben Jennings	Rutland SC	
2nd	Nicole Hemeryck	National YC	
3rd	Crispin Beaumont	Bartley SC	

2014		Pwllheli SC	204 entries
1st	Calum Rosie	Helensburgh SC	
2nd	Arran Holman	Hollowell SC	
3rd	Jack Butters	Parkstone YC	

2015		Weymouth	191 entries
1st	Joseph Drake	Royal Norfolk & S'folk	
2nd	Dylan Walendy-Wrigley	Harwich Town SC	
3rd	Niamh Harper	Loch Tummel SC	

NATIONAL CHAMPIONSHIPS REGATTA

FLEET WINNERS

2011		East Lothian YC
5.3	Oliver Martindale	Chew Valley Lake SC
4.2	Elliott Kuzyk	Parkstone YC

2012   Pwllheli SC
5.3 David Rosie   Helensburgh SC

2013   Weymouth
5.3 Rebecca Alcock   Hunts SC
4.2 James Fowler   Chew Valley Lake SC

2014   Pwllheli SC
5.3 Joseph Cohen   FOS SC
4.2 Zeb Fellows   Yealm YC

2015   Weymouth
5.3 Zeb Fellows   Yealm YC
4.2 George Vincent   Parkstone YC

INLAND CHAMPIOSHIP WINNERS

1983   Rutland Water SC   60 entries
1st Andrew Parr   Kingsmead SC
2nd Dave Parkinson   Elton SC
3rd Philip Allen   Walton on Thames SC

1984   Draycote Water SC
1st John Caig   Walton on Thames SC
2nd Tony Cooper   King George SC
3rd Jon Franklin   Maidenhead SC

1985   Rutland Water SC   87 entries
1st= Tony Prangnell   Hunts SC
1st= John Caig   Walton on Thames SC
3rd Chris Jones   Chew Valley Lake SC

1986   Bala SC   71 entries
1st   Andrew Peters   Bowmoor SC
2nd Tony Cooper   King George SC
3rd Anthony Bond   Hunts SC

1987   Grafham Water SC   106 entries
1st   Andrew Peters   Bowmoor SC
2nd Ashley Taylor   Christchurch SC
3rd Gordon Millar   Rutland Water SC

1988   Grafham Water SC   111 entries
1st   Tony Prangnell   Hunts SC
2nd Andrew Carter   Herne Bay SC
3rd John Caig   Walton on Thames SC

1989   Grafham Water SC   113 entries
1st   Graham Wright   Fenland SC
2nd Peter Keighley   Avon SC
3rd Tony Prangnell   Hunts SC

1990   Grafham Water SC   104 entries
1st   John Caig   Walton on Thames SC
2nd Tony Prangnell   Hunts SC
3rd Penny Mountford   Chelmarsh SC

1991   Grafham Water SC   113 entries
1st   Tim Wills   Grafham Water SC
2nd Gordon Miller   Rutland SC
3rd Paul Beale   Sutton SC

1992   Grafham Water SC   128 entries
1st Oliver Wells   Sheffield Viking SC
2nd Tim Wills   Grafham Water SC
3rd Graham Priestley   Ullswater YC

1993   Grafham Water SC   106 entries
1st Tim Wills   Grafham Water SC
2nd Stephen Cleland   Nelson Centre SC
3rd Dusty Miller   DeMontfort Uni SC

1994   Grafham Water SC   127 entries
1st Graham Priestley   Ullswater YC
2nd Chris Henderson   Sutton SC
3rd Edward Wright   Llyn Aled SC

1995   Grafham Water SC   151 entries
1st Mark Thirkettle   Craven SC
2nd Chris Henderson   Sutton SC
3rd Justin Deal   Chew Valley Lake SC

1996   Grafham Water SC   133 entries
1st Justin Deal   Chew Valley Lake SC
2nd Nicholas Bray   Broxbourne SC
3rd Tim Wills   Grafham Water SC

1997   Grafham Water SC   124 entries
1st Tim Wills   Grafham Water SC
2nd Tim Hulse   Ullswater YC
3rd Nicholas Bray   Broxbourne SC

1998   Grafham Water SC   136 entries
1st Tim Wills   Grafham Water SC
2nd Nick Lye   Crawley Mariners SC
3rd James Grant   West Lancs YC

1999   Grafham Water SC   146 entries
1st Ben McGrane   Chew Valley SC
2nd Andy Gatward   Melton Mowbray SC
3rd Anthony Bates   Ullswater YC

2000   Grafham Water SC   156 entries
1st Jackie Wilson   Ullswater YC
2nd Richard Peacock   Redditch SC
3rd Vincent Christian   Ely SC

2001   Grafham Water SC   193 entries
1st Giles Scott   Grafham Water SC
2nd Steven Hall   Hollowell SC
3rd Vincent Christian   Ely SC

2002   Grafham Water SC
1st Campbell Davidson Largs
2nd Steve Jackson   Hardway SC
3rd Chris Catt   Downs SC

2003   Grafham Water SC   267 entries
1st Daniel Belben   Stokes Bay SC
2nd Doug Horner   Wilsonian SC
3rd Steve Restall   Downs SC

2004 Grafham Water SC   263 entries
1st Thomas Gillard   Rotherham SC
2nd Thomas Dawber   Leigh & Lowton SC
3rd Eifion Mon   Red Wharf Bay SC

2005 Grafham Water SC
1st Eifion Mon   Red Wharf Bay SC
2nd Ben Palmer   Island Barn SC
3rd Adam Perry   South Staffs SC

2006 Grafham Water SC   239 entries
1st Bleddyn Mon   Red Wharf Bay SC
2nd Andrew Brown   Budworth SC
3rd Tom Weatherhead   Grafham Water SC

2007 Grafham Water SC   255 entries
1st Andrew Brown   Budworth SC
2nd Michael Wood   Draycote Water SC
3rd Phil McCoy   Emsworth Slipper SC

2008 Grafham Water SC   239 entries
1st Elliot Hanson   Redesmere SC
2nd Richard Cumpsty   Chew Valley Lake SC
3rd Andrew Dawson   Winsford Flash SC

2009 Grafham Water SC   260 entries
1st Peter Newbery   Earlswood Lakes SC
2nd Alexander Alcock   Hunts SC
3rd Christopher Eames   Strangford Lough SC

2010   Grafham Water SC   258 entries
1st   Kieren Hill   Scaling Dam SC
2nd Tobias Hamer   Langstone SC
3rd   Ellie Meopham   SolvaRowing&W'sports

2011   Grafham Water SC   246 entries
1st   Robbie Robinson   Plymouth Youth SC
2nd William Tarn-Chapman   Derwent Reservoir SC
3rd   Edward Connellan   Middle Nebe SC

2012   Grafham Water SC   213 entries
1st   Dan Venables   Sutton SC
2nd Nial Houston   Hayling Island SC
3rd   Felix Crowther   Hayling Island SC

2013   Grafham Water SC   178 entries
1st   Ben Jennings   Rutland SC
2nd Oliver Aldridge   Parkstone YC
3rd   Ben Whaley   Swanage SC

2014   Grafham Water SC   171 entries
1st   Calum Rosie   Helensburgh SC
2nd Lucy Mearns   Rhosneigr BOA
3rd   Elliott Kuzyk   Parkstone YC

2015   Grafham Water SC   153 entries
1st   Niamh Harper   Loch Tummel SC
2nd Joseph Drake   Royal Norfolk &S'folk
3rd   Billy Vennis-Ozanne   HHSC

WORLD CHAMPIONSHIP WINNERS

including * EUROPEAN CHAMPIONSHIPS

1979*   Clacton on Sea
1st   John Caig   Walton on Thames SC
2nd Bob Smolders   Holland
3rd   Patrik Mark   Sweden

1980*   Nessodden, Norway
1st   Bob Smolders   Holland
2nd Paul-Frederick Anderson   Norway
3rd   Kevin Moore   UK

1981*   Lac du Der, France
1st   Richard Perkins   Whitstable YC
2nd John Caig   Walton on ThamesSC
3rd   Ian Wright   Greenland Docks SC

1982   Paignton SC
1st   Ian Fryett   Chew Valley Lake SC
2nd Richard Perkins   Westbere FSA
3rd   John Caig   Walton on Thames SC

1984   Kristiansand, Norway
1st   Ian Fryett   Chew Valley Lake SC
2nd Andrew Rice   Walton on Thames SC
3rd   Richard Saxton   Yealm SC

1985 *   St. Catherine's SC, Jersey
1st   John Caig   Walton on Thames SC
2nd Ian Morrison   Channel Islands

3rd   Brian Worrall   Bowmoor SC

1986   Hellevoetsluis, Holland   76 entries
1st   Andrew Peters   Bowmoor SC
2nd Andrew Carter   Herne Bay SC
3rd   Barbara Hall   Chew Valley Lake SC

1987*   Thorpe Bay YC   117 entries
1st   Andrew Norman   Scaling Dam SC
2nd Andrew Carter   Herne Bay SC
3rd   Debbie Degge   Sandwell Valley SC

1988   Altmuhlsee, Germany   69 entries
1st   Andrew Carter   Herne Bay SC
2nd   Debbie Degge   Sandwell Valley SC
3rd   Elmar Rosemann   Germany

1989*   East Lothian YC   102 entries
1st   Jeremy Styles   Downs SC
2nd Andrew Carter   Herne Bay SC
3rd   Chris Reynolds   Locks SC

1990   Kantvikin YC, Finland   71 entries
1st   Debbie Degge   Sandwell Valley SC
2nd Tim Wills   Milton Keynes SC
3rd   Andrew Carter   Herne Bay SC

1992   Dummersee, Germany   97 entries
1st   Tim Wills   Grafham Water SC
2nd Stephen Cleland   Nelson Centre SC
3rd   Mikael Norberg   Sweden

1994   Helensburgh SC   153 entries

79

1st	Gordon Miller	Rutland SC
2nd	Austin Bailey	Bassenthwaite SC
3rd	Graham Priestley	Ullswater YC

1996   Dubai, UAE

1st	Neil Marsden	UK
2nd	Renee Smith	Australia
3rd	Cameron Miller	UAE

1998   Carnac, France

1st	Robert Carver	Jebel Ali, UAE
2nd	Tim Hulse	Ullswater YC
3rd	James Grant	West Lancs SC

2000   Cushendall YC

1st	Mark Heather	Wilsonian SC
2nd	Richard Peacock	Redditch SC
3rd	Andy Brooks	Elton SC

2002   Workum, Holland   132 entries

1st	Campbell Davidson	Largs
2nd	Chris Catt	Downs SC
3rd	Steve Jackson	Hardway SC

2004   Carnac, France   252 entries

1st	Eifion Mon	Red Wharf Bay SC
2nd	Craig Paul	Lochaber SC
3rd	Tom Dawber	Leigh & Lowton SC

2005*   Blessington SC, Ireland

1st	Bleddyn Mon	Red Wharf Bay SC
2nd	Thomas Gillard	Rotherham SC
3rd	Eifion Mon	Red Wharf Bay SC

2006   Fraglia Vela Malcesine, Italy 160 entries
1st Andrew Brown   Budworth SC
2nd Bleddyn Mon   Red Wharf Bay SC
3rd Michael Wood   Draycote Water SC

2008   Tralee Bay SC, Ireland   176 entries
1st Elliot Hanson   GBR
2nd Richard Cumpsty   GBR
3rd Jonathan Hewat   GBR

2009   Ebensee, Austria   94 entries
1st Andrew Bridgman   GBR
2nd Finn Lynch   GBR
3rd Felicity Foulds   GBR

2010   Fraglia Vela Malcseine, Italy 124 entries
1st Michele Benamati   ITA
2nd Giovanni Benamati   ITA
3rd Edward Jones   GBR

2011   Dun Loaghaire YC Dublin   174 entries
1st Matt Venables   GBR
2nd Robbie Robinson   GBR
3rd Patrick Crosbie   IRL

2012   Workum, Holland   141 entries
1st Giles Kuzyk   Parkstone YC
2nd Edward Higson   Frampton on Severn SC
3rd Felix Crowther   Hayling Island SC

2013   Cercle Nautique Loctudy, France103 entries
1st   Liam Glynn   IRL
2nd Thomas Wallwork   GBR
3rd   Georgie McKenzie   GBR

2014   Pwllheli SC   154 entries
1st   Calum Rosie   GBR
2nd Adam D'Arcy   IRL
3rd   Tom Walker   GBR

2015   Riva del Garda, Italy   156 entries
1st   Vittorio Gallinaro   ITA
2nd Patrick Zeni   ITA
3rd   Niamh Harper   GBR

NATIONWIDE TROPHY

1981	Jason Hughes	Draycote Water SC
1982	Richard Perkins	Westbere YC
1983	Jon Franklin	Maidenhead SC
1984	Debbie Degge	Sandwell Valley SC
1985	Paul Robinson	Papercourt SC
1986	Paul Robinson	Papercourt SC
1987	Paul Robinson	Papercourt SC

1988	Brian Worrall	Bowmoor SC
1989	Tim Garvin	Wraysbury Lake SC
1990	Paul Beale	Sutton SC
1991	Tim Wills	Grafham Water SC
1992	Graham Priestley	Ullswater SC
1993	Chris Henderson	Sutton SC
1994	John Burchell	Broxbourne SC
1995	Tim Wills	Grafham Water SC
1996	Andrew Gatward	Melton Mowbray SC
1997	Tim Hulse	Ullswater YC
1998	Andrew Gatward	Melton Mowbray SC
1999	Ben McGrane	Chew Valley Lake SC
2000	Stephen Wilson	Ullswater YC
2001	Giles Scott	Grafham Water SC
2002	James Stewardson	Ullswater YC
2003	Thomas Gillard	Rotherham SC

2004	Eifion Mon	Red Wharf Bay SC
2005	Bleddyn Mon	Red Wharf Bay SC
2006	Andrew Brown	Budworth SC
2007	Freddie Connor	Bexhill on Sea SC
2008	Elliot Hanson	Redesmere SC
2009	Michael Beckett	Solva R&W'Sports
2010	Robbie Robinson	Saltash SC
2011	Lawrence Logan	Nott'shire Co. SC
2012	Joseph Mullan	Priory SC
2013	Crispin Beaumont	Bartley SC
2014	Jack Butters	Parkstone YC

ORIGINAL ONE FLEET START TROPHIES

NATIONAL CHAMPIONSHIPS

Practice Race	Cobnor Cup
Race 1	Haulfryn Silver Trophy
Race 2	Commodore's Rose Bowl
Race 3	John Caig "Ace"
Race 4	Falcon Sailing Trophy
Race 5	Hyde One Design
Race 6	Topper International

Overall	Ian Proctor Trophy
1st Lady	Rose Bowl
1st Junior Male	ICI Trophy
1st Junior Female	Silver Cup
!st Senior Male	Tankard
1st Senior Female	Tankard
Endeavour	Shield
Optimo Parentis	Wooden Topper
Young Pretender U12	Shield

MULTIPLE FLEET START TROPHIES

NATIONAL CHAMPIONSHIPS

Overall	Ian Proctor Trophy
2nd Overall	Catrina Drummond Memorial
3rd Overall	GJW Cup
4th Overall	Hyde One Design
5th Overall	Trident
6th Overall	McVeigh Trophy
7th Overall	Cobner Clanger
Last Place Gold Fleet	Dixon Silver Salver
Last Race Winner Gold	Topper International
Gold Fleet 1st Female	Rose Bowl
Non Squad Junior Female	Silver Cup
Non Squad Junior Male	Silver Salver
Young Pretender U12	Shield
Endeavour	Shield
Most improved (last Nats)	Leapfrog
Optimo Parentis	Wooden Topper
1st Senior Male	Tankard
1st Senior Female	Tankard

85

First Nationals	Welcome Trophy
1st Kent Sailor	Jade Glass block
Race 3 Winner Gold Fleet	John Caig "Ace"

Silver Fleet 1st Overall	Commodore's Rose Bowl
2nd Overall	Donnie Meldrum
3rd Overall	Sailing Solutions Silver Sprint
4th Overall	Wet & Windy Tankard

Last Race Winner Silver	Green Slate Topper Class
Race 2 Winner Silver	Rooster
Race 5 Winner Silver	Scottish Toppers
Race 6 Winner Silver	Topper class
Race 8 Winner Silver	Topper Class

Bronze Fleet 1st Overall	Cupcake Cup
2nd Overall	Falcon
3rd Overall	Haulfryn Silver Topper

| 4.2 1st Overall | Summer Championship Trophy |
| 1st Youth | Perspex/Wooden Boat |

| Regatta Fleet 1st 4.2 | |
| Regatta fleet 5.3 | John Smalley Trophy |

OTHER TROPHIES

| Winter Regatta 1st Male | ICOM Cup |
| Winter Regatta 1st Female | Brassington Claret Jug |

Inland Championships
1st Overall
1st Junior
1st Female
1st Junior Female
1st 4.2 sailor

4.2 Championships
1st 4.2 Squad Sailor   Dixon Salver
1st Female   Pewter Dinghy on shield
1st Overall   Sailing Solutions Topper

Autumn Event
1st U14 Boy Sept NS Event   Cathy Cunnison Salver
1st U14 Girl Sept NS Event   Craftinsure Rose Bowl

INDEX